The "true book" series is prepared

under the direction of

Illa Podendorf

Laboratory School, University of Chicago

Ninety-eight per cent of the text is in words from

the *Combined Word List for Primary Reading*

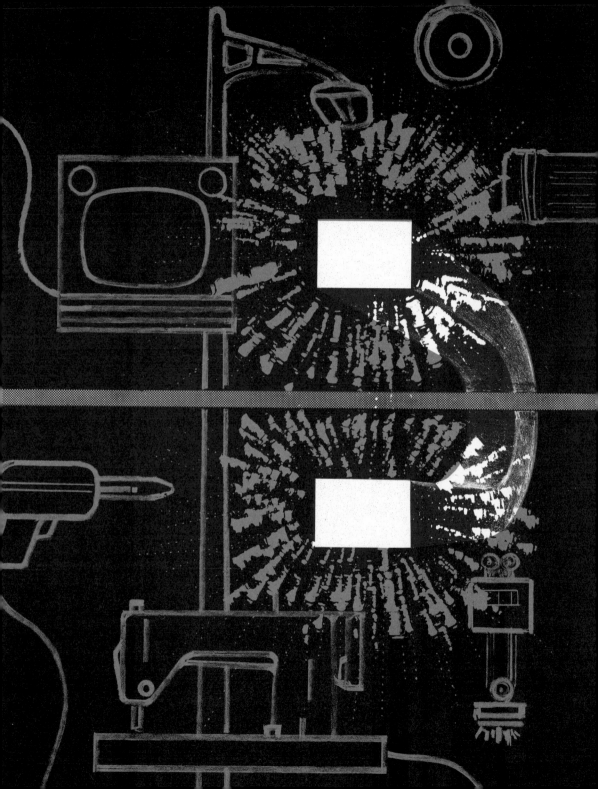

the true book of

MAGNETS and ELECTRICITY

By ILLA PODENDORF
Pictures by ROBERT BORJA

CHILDRENS PRESS, CHICAGO

CONTENTS

Library of Congress Catalog Card No. 61-10094

THIS EDITION PRINTED 1965

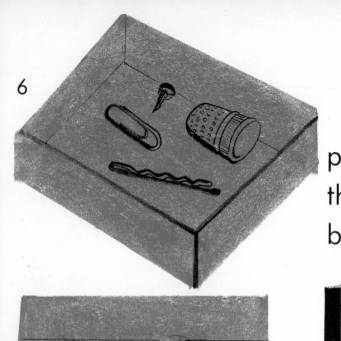

Magnets will pick up every-thing in this box.

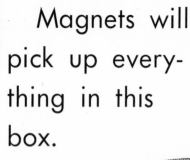

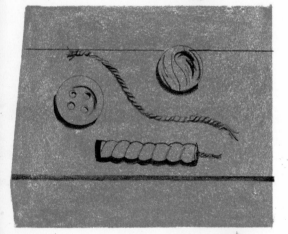

They will pick up nothing in this box.

Magnets will pick up some of the things in this box. Magnets will pick up things made of iron or steel.

Sometimes magnets
will pull
toward each other.

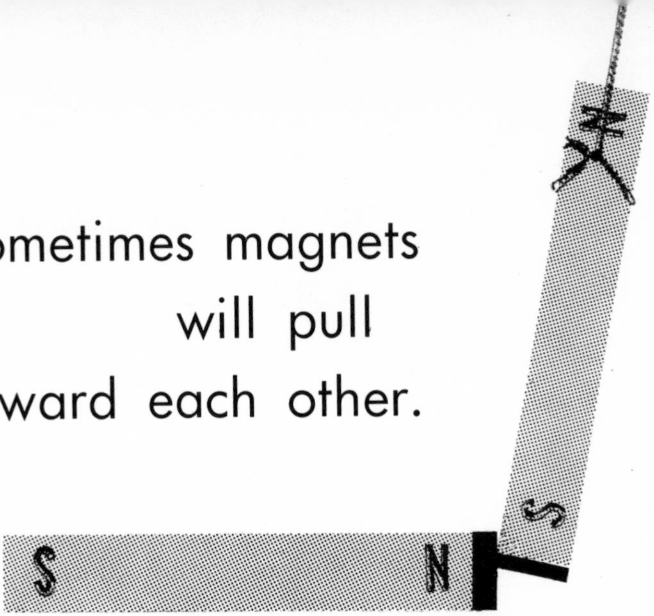

S   N S

Sometimes
magnets will push away
from each other.

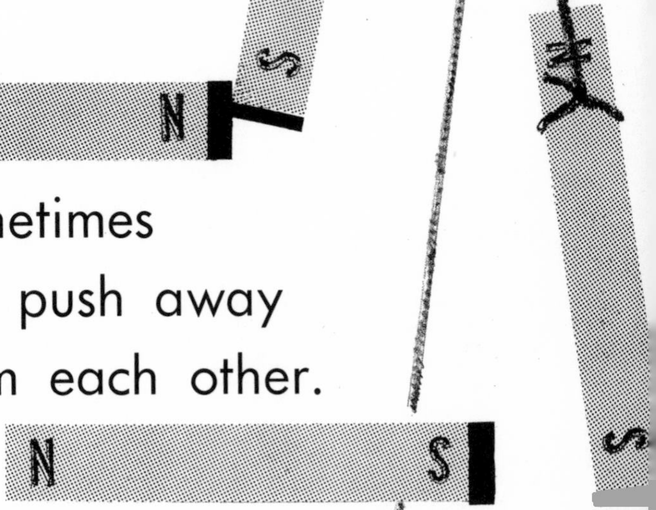

N   S

Now they are
pulling toward
each other again.

S   N S

7

The ends of the magnets are called poles. One end is a north-seeking pole. The other end is a south-seeking pole.

Hang a bar magnet so that it can swing freely. The north-seeking pole will point toward the north. The south-seeking pole will point toward the south.

The north-seeking pole of a magnet is called the "N" pole.

The south-seeking pole of a magnet is called the "S" pole.

N   S

If the N pole of one magnet
is held toward the S pole
of another, the magnets will
pull toward each other.

N   S   N

The S pole of one magnet
will push away from the
S pole of another magnet.

S   S   N

The N pole of one magnet will push
away from the N pole of another magnet.

S   N

N

S

Remember: Poles which are alike
push away from each other.
Poles which are not alike,
          pull together.

This is why one magnet will
sometimes pick up another magnet
and why sometimes it will not.

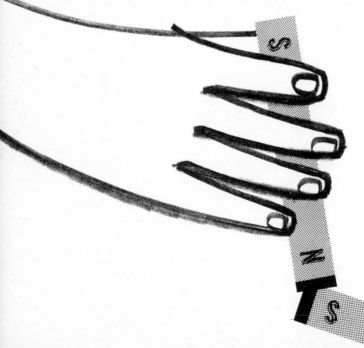

You may wonder why the
magnet's poles point north
and south. This is because
the earth has two magnetic poles
which attract the poles of
your magnet.

This paper boat can be made to move over glass with a magnet. The boat has a paper clip on it. A magnet will pull on the paper clip through the glass.

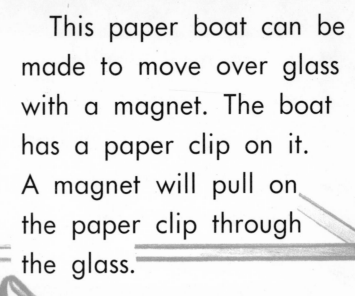

Magnets will pull through air, too. A paper clip on a string will stay in the air if the pull of the magnet is strong enough. The clip is in the magnet's "magnetic field."

There are tiny bits of iron on this paper. The magnet pulls on them. The magnet pulls on them because they are in the magnet's magnetic field, and the magnet will pull through paper.

The magnet pulls on the iron bits even though it does not touch them or the paper.

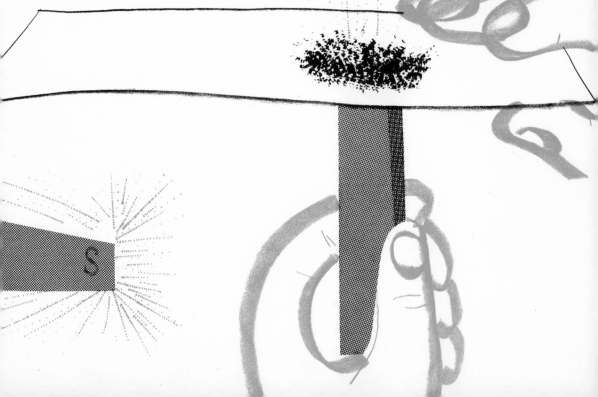

Magnets are of many different shapes.

Does a round magnet have poles? Use a bar magnet and find out.

All magnets have poles. All
magnets have magnetic fields.

Some magnets are stronger
than others. We cannot tell
by the size of a magnet how
strong it is.

Where are magnets
the strongest? Here
is an experiment
that shows that
they are strongest
at their poles.

If a magnet is broken, then each half will have an N pole and an S pole.

We should take good care of magnets.

We should not drop them,

should not pound them,

should not heat them.

Magnets should be put away with keepers.

Magnets should be put away with S and N poles together.

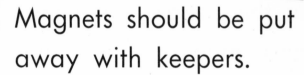

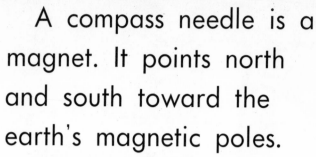

A compass needle is a magnet. It points north and south toward the earth's magnetic poles. You can make a needle into a compass. Hold a magnet in one hand, and a steel needle in the other hand. Rub the needle from one end of the magnet to the other, about fifty times. Always hold the needle in the same way and rub it on the magnet in the same direction.

Lay the needle on a cork. Float the cork in water. The needle will point north and south.

Hang a needle from a thread in a glass jar. The needle will pull through the glass and point north and south. Make other compasses.

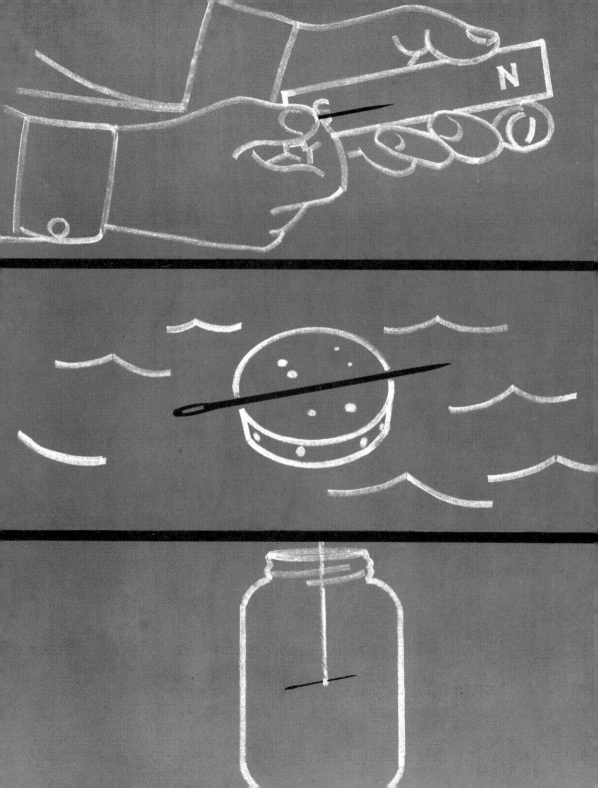

Magnets can
be used to pick
up things from
queer places.

They can be
used to sort
things.

They are
used in beauty
parlors.

The magnets you have been
reading about cannot be
turned off and on. They are
called "permanent magnets."
Electric magnets are magnets
only when electricity is
going through them.

You can make an
electric magnet with
1 dry cell,

1 iron bolt about 2 inches long,

5 yards of number 24 cotton-
covered copper wire.

Cut off one yard of the wire.
Save it to use later.

Start at one end of the bolt
and about one foot from the end
of the long piece of wire.

Wrap the wire around the bolt.
Wrap carefully from one end of
the bolt to the other. Turn
around and wrap back again.

Keep wrapping until almost
all of the wire has been used.
Leave one foot at each end of
the wire to use for connections.
Twist the two wires together so
that the wire on the bolt will
not come loose.

Connect one wire to each of
the posts of the dry cell.
Do you have a magnet?
Your magnet should pick up
things made of iron and steel.

Take one wire off of the
dry cell. Your magnet will drop
its load. This is the way to
turn your magnet off and on again.

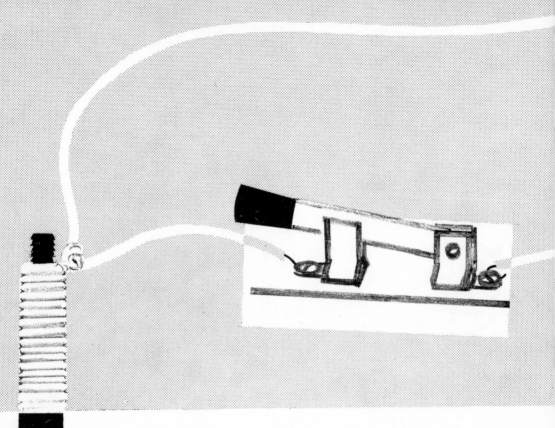

If you use a switch and a
piece of the wire which you
saved, you can make it easier
to turn your magnet off and on.

To make your electric magnet
stronger, add another dry cell.

When you connect two dry cells

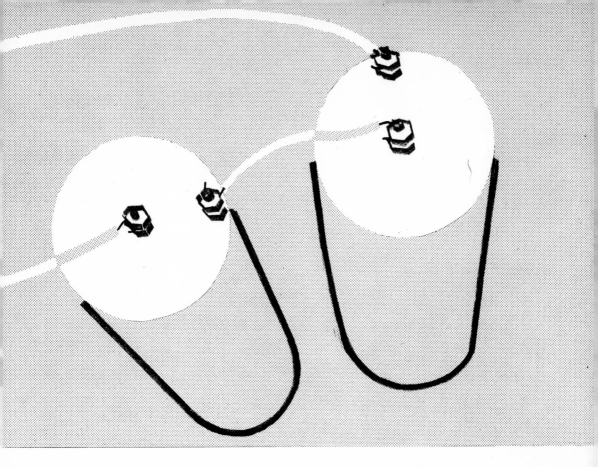

be sure you connect the inside
post on one dry cell to the out-
side post of the other.

There is another way to make
electric magnets stronger. Wrap
more wire around the iron bolt.

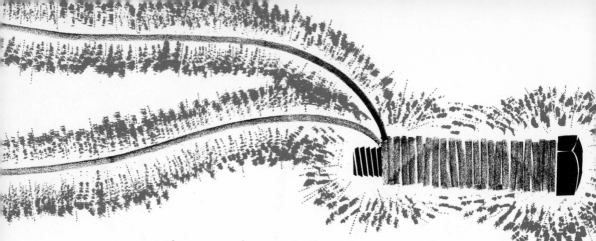

When electricity goes through
a wire, a magnetic field is made
around the wire. The iron bolt
becomes a magnet. The magnetic
field is gone when the electricity
is turned off. The iron bolt is
no longer a magnet. Iron loses
its magnetic pull quickly.

A steel bolt would not lose
its pull quickly and then could
not be turned off. This is why
an iron bolt is used to make an
electric magnet.

Big electric
magnets are
used to lift
heavy loads.

Electric magnets
are used to lift
things from under
water.

They are used
to clean streets.

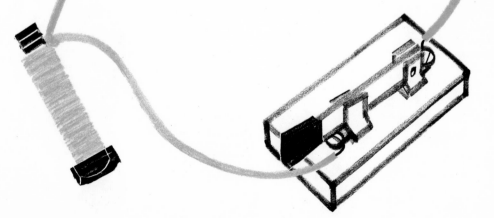

There must be a
complete circuit to make
your electric magnet work.
It must be possible for the
electricity to go from one
post of the dry cell
through all of the wires
to the other post of
the dry cell.

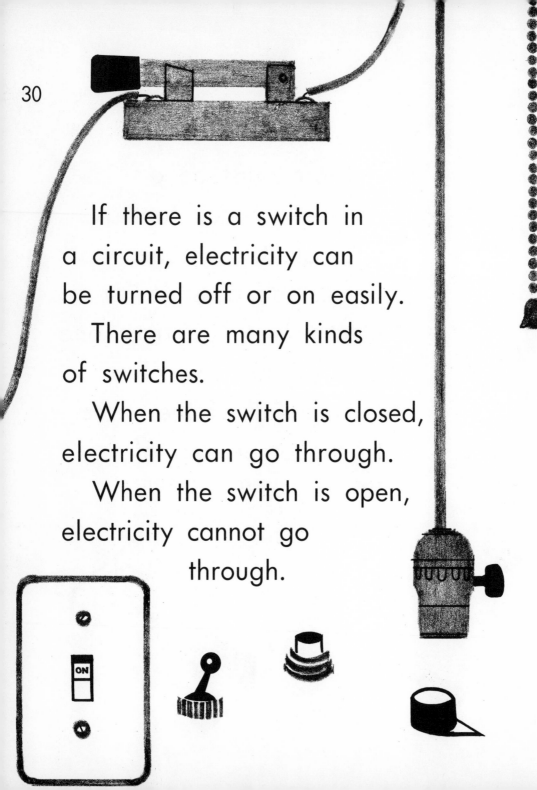

If there is a switch in
a circuit, electricity can
be turned off or on easily.
   There are many kinds
of switches.
   When the switch is closed,
electricity can go through.
   When the switch is open,
electricity cannot go
                through.

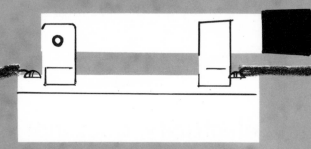

When a switch is open, we
say the circuit is broken.
Circuits are broken in
other ways, too.
A wire may break, or there
might be a loose
connection.

When electricity does not
follow the circuit but goes
an easier path, it is called
a short circuit.

A short circuit can be
dangerous. It may cause
a fire.

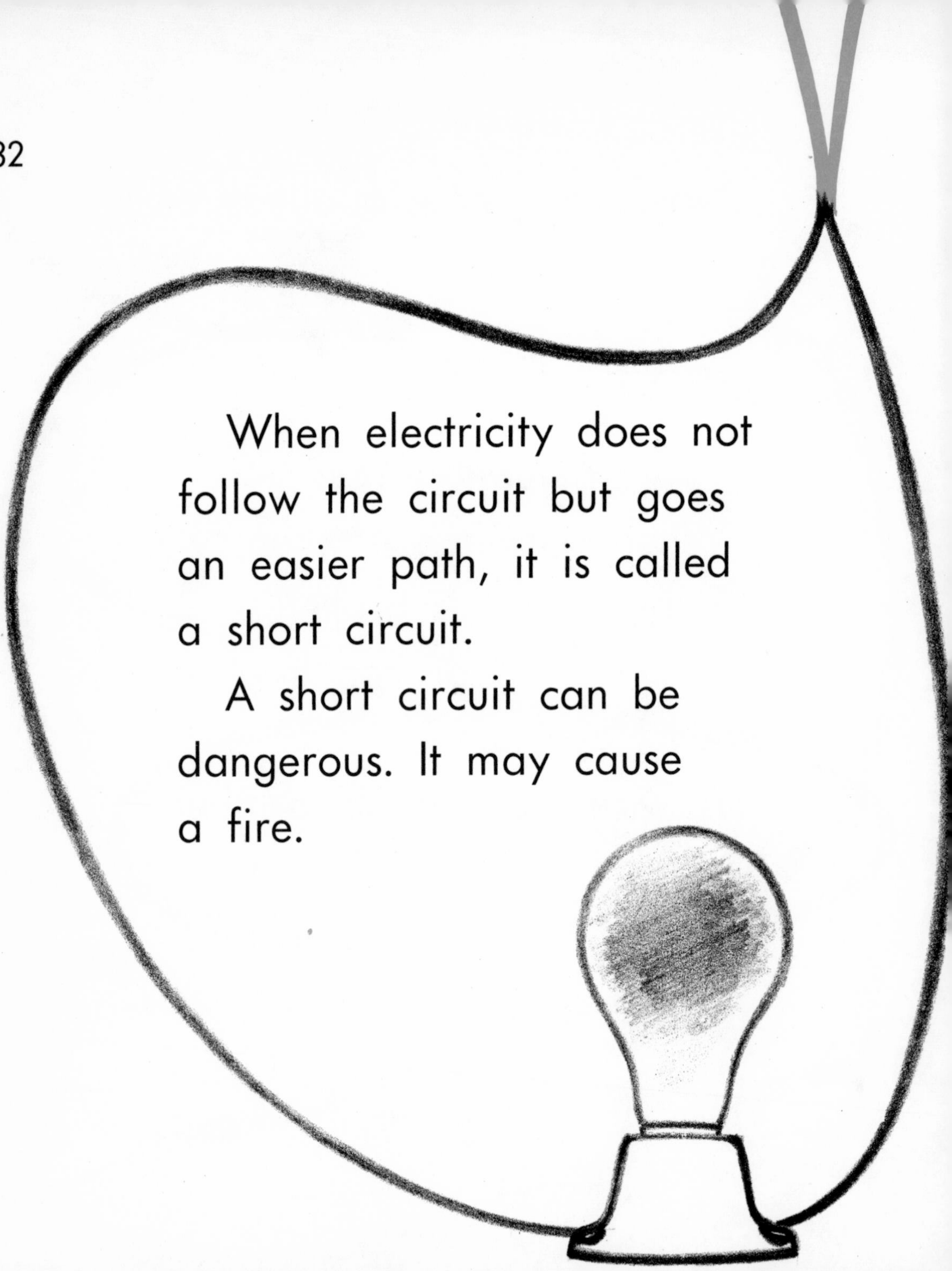

Now you know about three circuits.

Complete circuit.

Broken circuit.

Short circuit.

Electricity is useful.

We cook with it.

We light our
homes and streets
with it.

We would have no radio or television without electricity.

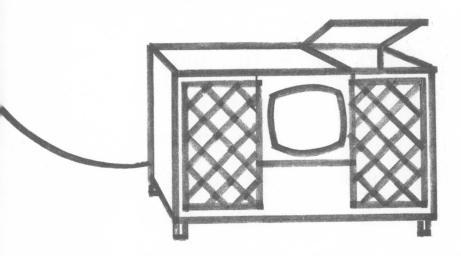

We may heat our homes with it.

We do work with it.

Electricity can be dangerous when it goes where we do not want it to go. A fire may start from it. A person might get a shock from it.

The covering on wires helps keep electricity on the right path. If the covering on the wire is torn or broken, the electricity may go where it is not wanted.

Some things are called good
conductors because electricity
goes through them well.

Electricity will not travel
through some things.

Wires which carry electricity
must be good conductors.

The covering on the wires
is made of something through
which electricity will not
travel. This covering is
called insulation.

An electric wire is dangerous
if the insulation is not good.

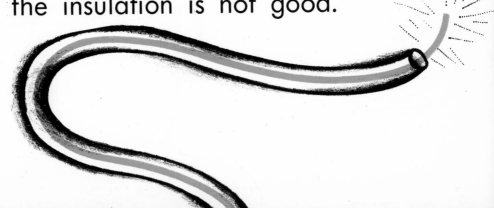

Most metals are conductors
of electricity.

Paper, string, rubber and
other things will not conduct
electricity.

Since metals are conductors of electricity, never touch a piece of metal that electricity might be going through.

Never touch an electric wire which is broken or hanging down.

Never play with electricity which comes through wall sockets. It is much too strong for play.

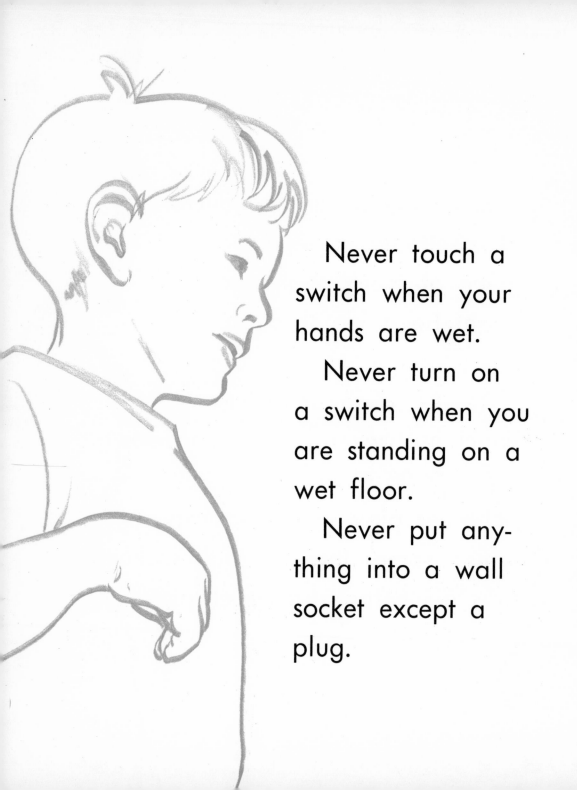

Never touch a switch when your hands are wet.

Never turn on a switch when you are standing on a wet floor.

Never put any-thing into a wall socket except a plug.

You have been
reading about
"current" electricity.

Lightning is
"static" electricity.

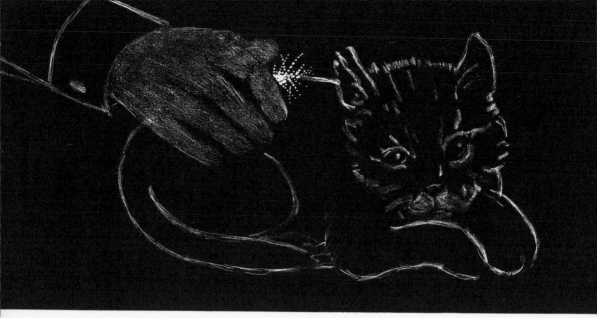

If you take a kitten to a dark room and rub its fur, you may see sparks. The sparks are static electricity.

Rub your feet over a rug and touch something. You may feel static electricity.

You may see and hear
static electricity on
a cold day when you
comb your hair with
a rubber comb.

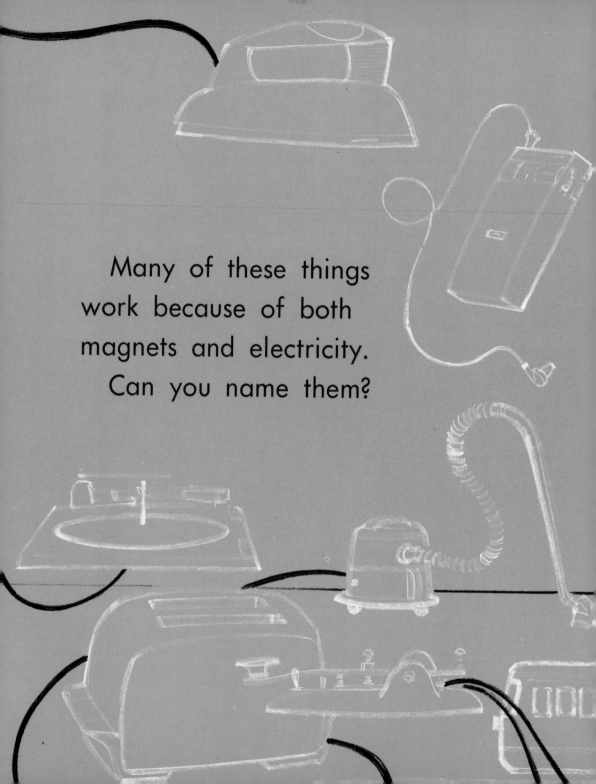

Many of these things
work because of both
magnets and electricity.
Can you name them?

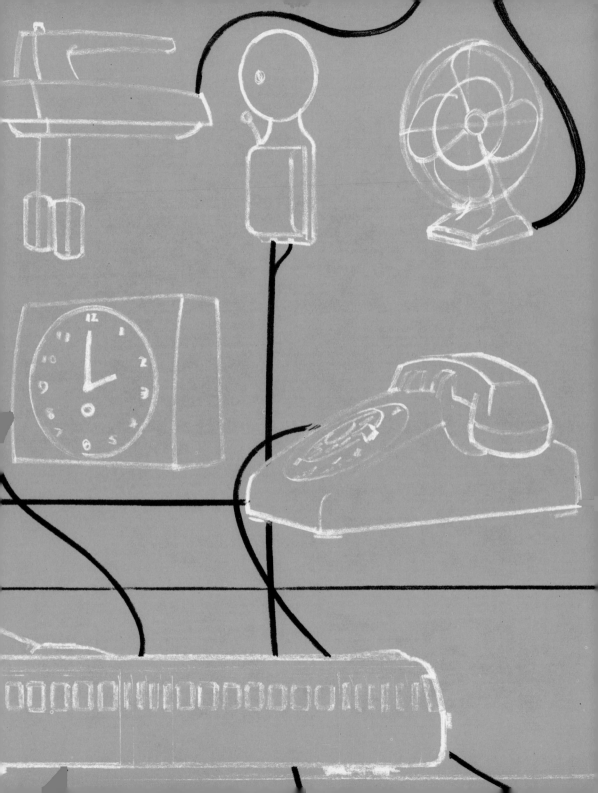

NOW
YOU
KNOW

1. Magnets will attract things made of iron or steel.

2. Magnets work by the laws of their poles.

3. Magnets will pull through things which they do not attract.

4. Magnets are strongest at their poles.

5. Magnets are of many different shapes.

6. Some magnets are stronger than others.

7. Permanent magnets are very useful.

8. Magnets have a field of force around them.

9. Electric magnets can be turned off and on.

10. Electric magnets can be made stronger.

11. Electric magnets are very useful.

12. Electric circuits must be complete for electricity to go through.

13. Some things are better conductors of electricity than others.

14. Electricity is very useful.

15. Electricity can be very dangerous.

16. Static electricity can be made by rubbing.

17. There is a magnetic field around wires with electricity going through them.

18. Many things work because of both magnets and electricity.

1. Find as many different magnets as you can and do some of the things which you read about in this book.

2. Make a compass.

3. Make an electric magnet.

4. Make your electric magnet stronger.

THINGS TO DO

5. Test your electric magnet and find out whether it has poles.

6. Try changing the poles of your electric magnet by changing the wires on the posts of the dry cell from one post to the other.

7. Make a switch with a small strip of copper, a wooden block, and a couple of thumb tacks.

8. Use a dry cell and some wire and use the switch you made in number 7 in a complete circuit.

9. Make a collection of pictures to show the uses of electricity.

10. Make a set of safety rules to follow when you use electricity.